In
Search
Of
Eden

IN SEARCH OF EDEN

Understanding
New Age Thought

DAVID J. FELTER

BEACON HILL PRESS OF KANSAS CITY
KANSAS CITY, MISSOURI

Copyright 1991
by Beacon Hill Press of Kansas City

ISBN: 083-411-4089

Printed in the
United States of America

Cover Design: Crandall Vail
Cover Illustration: Royce Ratcliff

All scriptures quoted are from the King James Version
of the Bible.

10   9   8   7   6   5   4   3   2   1

Dedication

To Sandy, God's gift to me;
and to David and Pam, and Jib and LeEtta,
God's blessings to me

Contents

Preface

I received a letter from a lady in New England in which she stated, "I have heard of [the New Age movement] but know very little about [it.] I would like to know more." What follows is my attempt to state briefly, and succinctly, the major elements of New Age thought.

There are many books that describe facets of the New Age movement. Some are quite detailed, while others suggest a New Age conspiracy lurks behind every new idea we hear. This work tries to steer a middle course.

There is much in the New Age movement that is deplorable, even dangerous. There are also some insights that may prove useful as they are separated from the bizarre and refined over time. You can be the judge of that.

What is important is that we understand clearly the foundation on which most of New Age thought rests. This work is far from exhaustive. The writer has tried to ferret out the major foundations underlying the most frequently encountered strands of this phenomenon. These have been compared with the normative statements of the Bible. You can judge whether they (elements of New Age thought) are suitable for incorporation in your everyday living.

It was not the writer's purpose to provide a list of suspect activities, books, writers, music, etc. The primary objective has been to provide a basic understanding of the critical differences between New Age thought and normative Christianity. If the reader grasps this, he will be in a position to properly evaluate subsequent experiences and encounters with this yardstick.

To those interested in further study, the titles referred to in the Bibliography will provide fertile ground for such a pursuit.

1

The Attraction of New Age Thought

I settled back in my seat to await takeoff from Kansas City International Airport en route to Philadelphia. In those first few minutes before departure, I go through a mental checklist:

1. Are my tithes all paid and up-to-date?
2. Did I have my personal devotions this morning?
3. Did I leave my wife with a kind word?
4. Is there anything between me and God?
5. Did I look at the pilot, and did he look as if he was sober?

Then I start to pray. I pray for the cabin crew. I pray about the weather. I pray for the engines. I pray for a good takeoff.

I'm not scared of flying. I just like to use my spare time for quiet conversations with God. And just before takeoff is one of those excellent opportunities.

At 33,000 feet, I reflected on my assignment in Philadelphia. I was going there as a representative of my church to a special clergy conference. I was anxious to attend and was looking forward to the experience.

About 50 miles out of Philadelphia, I had another one of those excellent opportunities for a quiet conversation with the Lord. Landing always helps me put my life in its most appropriate perspective.

After registering and settling into my room, I looked over the program of the conference. The first item after dinner was a devotional time for all conferees. I thought, Great! This will be a wonderful way to get started. Little did I know I was about to encounter my first experience with New Age thought.

I found my way to the room for the devotional and took a seat. I noticed a pleasant-faced man at the front of the room with a small lectern and a cassette recorder.

I thought, Oh no! I hope we're not going to have to sing "Kum-ba-yah" or some other song I probably don't know.

He stood silently before us. The silence filled the room. In a quiet, measured voice, he said:

"I want you all to relax. Go deep into your spirit," he said.

The idea, he told us, was to put away all the noise of the hours preceding our arrival. We were to cleanse our minds of the clutter that makes learning and spiritual communion difficult. By relaxing our muscles and breathing deeply, we would begin to meditate. He instructed us to focus our thoughts on a mysterious spot in our bodies that would serve as the center of our physical existence. By focusing there, we could concentrate our minds and focus on something specific rather than letting our minds run like an idling motor.

To accompany the exercise, he played a cassette tape of Pachelbel's *Canon*. This is a beautiful piece of classical music with a haunting, repetitious melody line. It is easy to listen to and has a sort of hypnotic effect, calming the senses. To this accompaniment, the speaker began guiding our meditation.

At first we were to concentrate on our physical relaxation. Sitting straight on metal chairs, we were told to place our hands on our knees, letting our heads droop gently until we were quite limp. The beautiful strings of the violins played the melody over and over.

The speaker gently spoke of "letting go." Quite frankly, it was a relaxing experience. I tried to focus on the center of my body, concentrating all my energy in one spot. Even at this point, I was still fairly comfortable with my experience so far. Meditation was not something I regularly practiced, but I had read Richard Foster's *Celebration of Discipline* with its instructions: "Another meditation aimed at centering oneself begins by concentrating on breathing. Having seated yourself comfortably, slowly become conscious of your breathing. This will help you get in touch with your body and indicate to you the level of tension within."[1]

After several minutes of listening to the music, allowing our bodies to drain away the tension, our speaker began.

"God is like an opera singer," he said. "He sings this note (my existence), but I keep muting the note. The question for me is, 'What is the nature of my note?'"

Even though I was deeply relaxed, my mind tried to deal with this statement. What does this mean? I thought. The speaker told us to think of all the notes that were in the music we were listening to. He told us to imagine them as the creation of God, flowing out from Him in beauty and uniqueness.

Our speaker told us that many of us tried to mute our note; that through the experiences of our lives, we had grown to dislike our note. We wanted to be some other note. And, because we couldn't be that note, we muted our note instead of letting it ring out as it was intended by God.

The purpose of meditation and relaxation was to help us silence our inner voice, calming our actions and stilling our conflict. In order to consider the purpose of our existence and the nature of our identity, we must first center our consciousness.

"When you're ready," he said, "you can come back."

Slowly I opened my eyes. My body had become as relaxed as a Maytag repairman. Deep peace seemed to flood my being. I felt suspended in a calm serenity. Although I didn't know any of the conferees, I felt a warmth of collegiality.

It all sounds pretty harmless, doesn't it? And it seemed harmless to me at the time, although I must admit I was having difficulty with the speaker's notion of God as an opera singer.

The next devotional period was led by a different gentleman. His approach took us down a different road. No quiet music this time. No deep meditation or visualization exercises.

Our leader began by speaking about the critical issues of our lives. He talked about four things, according to his research, that each one of us had encountered.

He said there are four principles into which we keep bumping as we go through life:

1. The principle of uncertainty
2. The principle of multiple polarities
3. The principle of dissipative structures
4. The principle of complementarity

I thought, That's heavy duty. I wonder what that means in simple English?

I didn't have to wait long.

He said, "Nothing is ever certain in life. If you put all your eggs in one basket, you may be disappointed."

Clear enough, I thought. What's next?

"The next one," he said, "is not quite as clear as the first.

"We have been trained to go through life seeing only two polarities, positive and negative, good or evil, or black and white. If this is the paradigm of your life, you will encounter problems in your dealings with others.

"Worse yet," he said, "we all have to live and deal with others who see life and its structures from the same limitations we share."

At this point, my mind was beginning to feel that same vibrating sensation one gets when walking in a crowded shopping mall on the second level and the floor seems to shake. It seemed that our speakers were directing us to think less of the solid, somewhat tangible foundations of our lives, and to open up to the less-tangible idea of free-floating realities. Maybe it was just a holdover from the days of my conservative upbringing, but whatever it was, I was beginning to feel uneasy. Red flags began waving. Bells were going off in my brain.

I thought, Well, I'm this far in, I may as well stick around to hear the rest of the story.

I figured I knew a little about the principle of dissipative structures. The speaker said, "Things are not always going to be the way they are now, in your life. Things are changing even as we speak. Relationships change, bodies age, abilities fail, opportunities deteriorate."

It really didn't take much genius to figure this one out. When we are young, we think things will last forever, never changing, always staying the same. But, as Thomas Wolfe once wrote, "You can never go home again."

The last principle was the one about complementarity. Frankly, I didn't have a clue as to what he was talking about. I listened closely to his explanation.

"This principle is in effect," he said, "when you are unable to see possibility B for looking at reality A." In other words, you can't see the woods for the trees. I knew that complement could be defined as "something added to complete a whole."[2]

Apparently our speaker was trying to tell us that we need something more to complete us. What I didn't grasp at the time was the fact that this "something more" was our own inner divinity. Because of my implicit faith and trust in

God, I was not nearly as open to suggestions concerning my own divinity as were some of my colleagues in the room.

The speaker then summed up his address:

———

If your life is your calling, you are never out of work.

Always remember, life works, just as the universe keeps perpetuating itself.

No despair of yours can destroy the reality of who you are.

Within you is the power to excel in your life.

———

It suddenly dawned on me that I was listening to the appeal of New Age thought. It was now beginning to make sense. My calling was not my life, my life only expressed my calling. Our speaker was telling us that we should look inward, not outward to the source of our calling.

As for his conviction that life works, just like the universe, well, my experience didn't confirm his findings. I thought, If life always works, just like the universe, then life is nothing more than some mechanical puzzle, put together by some unfeeling intelligence.

How can one tell the crippled boy, watching his friends play ball, "Son, just remember, life always works just like the universe." What a cold thought! There is no comfort in that idea. Perhaps that crippled boy may be too young to know, but soon he will learn that the universe is flawed. It works, but only in the cold reality of mathematical laws. It would just as soon hurl meteors in devastating power toward other planets as it would awaken sleeping flowers in the spring earth.

Even with its coldness, New Age thought has a subtle, yet strong, attraction for our times. We are the inheritors of the postindustrial age. Our grandparents and our parents transformed our world into a cornucopia of infinite opportunities and passed it on down to us. Now, most of us live free from the grinding tyranny of traditional work. Oh, we work, all right; we live by exchanging, trading, accumulating, or creating information. Even industry is freeing employees from routine and demanding physical labor through robotics and smart machines.

Yet in the midst of unprecedented progress, technology, and affluence, we live with demons. We live with the ugly monsters of child abuse, spousal abuse, parental abuse, substance abuse, and a thousand other abuses.

Fewer of us live near the land. Our escapes to nature take place in parks or nature preserves. Daily we hear the tragic stories of the rape of nature. Oil spills, acid rain, and pollution compete with other stories on the nightly news.

We struggle with dwarfed self-esteem, poor self-images, and nameless, faceless fears. Our inner peace is robbed by the abrasive stress of modern life. Our pace is accelerating, yet the certainty of our destiny is blurring.

For some, cynicism is slowly overtaking them. The Church, once a refuge and stronghold of the faith, now disappoints them. With the permissiveness of frank candor, they question the warts and wrinkles on the face of the Church. Slowly this creeping cynicism erodes commitment, and faith dies. Like locusts shedding old skins, we leave our faith, while our empty carcasses remain anchored to the branches of the tree. We are in the Church, but not of it.

Baby boomers have watched faith become mere perfunctory performance in the lives of their parents. They have watched it become a discarded relic. Their own spiritual hunger gnaws at their inner being. Their search for answers to the disquieting questions of self-identity and self-worth has lead them from heavy metal music, drug experimentation, and promiscuous sexuality to life-styles of insatiable consumerism. In this vacuum New Age thought is making tremendous inroads.

Robbed of the warm spirituality of a living relationship with God, many people turn to the cold, mechanical universe for answers to their pressing problems. They have discovered their own emotional bankruptcy. They long for the warmth; instead they feel only the cold. Talk of rainbows, spiritual encounters with nature, and exchanging energy with a group seems appealing in light of the emotional refrigerator in which they live.

What is the appeal of New Age thought? One might think that some of its bizarre proponents like Shirley MacLaine would turn off thinking people. Is that true? Not quite. Because most of us are not students of history, we fail to understand the lengths to which seemingly civilized people will go to find meaning for their lives. New Age thought proposes a meaning built out of the experiences of everyday life. Further on we shall see that New Age thought is not linked to anything external at all. Its foundation is the inner experiences of its participants, including the bizarre kaleidoscopic images of trance channelers, crystal merchants, and native peoples' magic.

At the conference I attended, the speaker spoke of the *principle of multiple polarities.* What does this mean, and what is its significance concerning New Age thought?

We are confronted with dual polarities every day. The electrician wiring our houses knows that every circuit must have a positive and negative side. Current will not flow unless these polarities are correctly observed. In our everyday speech, we talk about things that are "black and white." By this we understand that the opposite positions are clearly evident to us.

For the Christian, there is a clear, biblical understanding of the polarities of good and evil, sin and righteousness, heaven and hell. We also know there are "gray" areas in which the black and white of certainty are difficult to distinguish. For us, however, the moral realm is not a sliding scale or a gray area with many different shadings. The bedrock of our behavioral guidance stems from our understanding of the Ten Commandments as the infallible and unchanging law of God.

In New Age thought there is room for more than two polarities. The term *polarity* comes from the idea of two poles that cap the top and bottom of our globe. While east and west is a continuum that blurs—i.e., at some invisible point east becomes west and vice versa—the polar regions of our planet are well-defined. In electrical current, if the polarities, i.e., positive or negative, are reversed, a fuse will blow, and the circuit will no longer carry electricity.

New Age thought suggests that the issues of life are not always as clear and simple as are the laws of electricity. To this argument we agree. It is often difficult to discover the certainty of black and white. We are confronted with varying shades of gray. New Age thought believes that in such situations there are more than just one, two, or even three ways of looking at them. In fact, according to New Age thought, trying to fit circumstances and situations into just two categories, e.g., right and wrong, if not impossible, is not always right for you.

The educational system in which many of our children participate corroborates this idea. It suggests *there is no single right or wrong way of doing things.* According to this principle, there are ways of doing things that may be better or worse than others. To suggest that one is right and the other wrong is, according to New Age teaching, to believe in a helplessly outmoded dualism.

If one were to draw a line representing traditional thinking versus New Age thinking, it would look like this:

DUALISM_____MULTIPLE POLARITIES

According to New Age thinkers, Christians are locked into a outdated and outmoded dualism. What is dualism? It

is the idea that the world is ultimately made up of two opposite forces, e.g., good and evil. While this is an over-
simplified definition, it illustrates the basic difference between Christianity and New Age thought.

New Age thought believes that the discoveries of
physics concerning the basic nature of reality no longer
permit a dualistic view of the universe. The new physics
describe the essence of all things to be pure energy, rather
than a combination of matter and energy. In a world where
everything could be reduced to either matter or energy, dualism made sense. In a world where all existence can be
defined as the expression of some form of energy, dualism
is outmoded, the New Agers say.

If the idea of absolute right and absolute wrong can no
longer be held by intelligent, thinking people, what can
they believe? The answer, say New Agers, is to be found in
multiple polarities, multiple ways of doing things, no absolute wrong or absolute right. There is only a continuum
that stretches endlessly. Any position on that continuum is
permissible. The only criterion is whether or not it works
for you.

For many, this falls on welcome ears. Much of humanity sees the unyielding rigidity of the Judeo-Christian absolutes as intolerable. Yet, their spiritual hunger continues.
And to satisfy this God-given hunger, they turn to New
Age thought.

New Age thought overlooks the obvious in search of
the obscure. If there are multiple polarities and everyone is
right and no one is wrong, what's to prevent a disin-
tegrating explosion of clashing wills and conflicting values?
For the Christian, there is a great deal of difference between finding shades of meaning and value on the spectrum of human experience and the idea of many different
points of view, all equally correct. Just think of the havoc
that would occur if mathematicians were to suddenly say,
"Two plus two no longer equals four. It can add up any way

you want it to. It now represents whatever value you give it."

It is more difficult to accept the idea of only two polarities as opposed to multiple polarities. If a behavior or event consists of the value I give it, I make myself in charge of the universe. I answer only to myself. It allows me freedom to determine the moral value of events and behaviors. I am vested with the formulas for determining right and wrong. In the end, a behavior becomes right or wrong for me only in relation to what I want. If a behavior assists me in getting what I want, it is right. If a behavior detracts me from my goal (I am also able to determine the moral legitimacy of my goals), it is wrong.

While this is another oversimplification for the sake of illustration, it does point out the basic philosophy of New Age thought.

New Age thought is trumpeted as "home to a multitude of voices from the present and the past (prophets, poets, theologians, scientists, native peoples, mystics, and activists), who know that the richest, most dramatic revelation of spiritual truth is to be found in the cosmos itself."[3]

Another source says, "It is a forum for the kind of spirituality that can help sustain, rather than destroy, the earth; a spirituality of creativity, generative, earthiness, celebration and wholeness."[4]

It is important that we not dismiss New Age thought as the province of eccentrics like Shirley MacLaine, and Hollywood celebrities who practice channeling and use crystals. Clearly, dismissing New Age thought as the stomping grounds of weirdos from la-la land prevents us from seeing both its potential and its threat.

Why do people get involved in New Age thought? Maurice Smith writes the following:

1. For some individuals, the dominant Christian view has broken down, or the church as they have known it has

disappointed them. They may turn to [anything] as [a] substitute religion that satisfies deeply felt needs.

2. In our modern, postindustrial society, people may feel baffled, not safe anymore. For some an alternative reality is appealing, a sort of counterculture religion.

3. New Age thinking offers many a way to get power over their lives, a handle on their situation. New Age movements stress human effort, human potential, and human perfectibility.

4. Much of the interest in New Age thinking is faddish.

5. New Age thought offers an alternate style of religion in which people are offered ways to reject their traditions and assert what they think is their own independence.

6. Many New Agers think the church is irrelevant, inadequate, and even unnecessary. They find special pleasure in an intellectual, self-help avenue to religion and in the security of an exclusive group.

7. New Age ideas appear as secular approaches to problem solving. One can embrace New Age ideas without joining a church. There are no rigid rules of behavior, no authoritative book, no prescribed doctrines, no sermons on sin, and no necessary public commitment.[5]

Many religious movements are reactions. New Age thought is a reaction, not a consistent or systematic body of philosophy or theology. It is an approach born out of a reaction against forces that dehumanize humanity and destroy natural environments. New Age thinkers are not all clustered in Vail, Colo., singing John Denver songs. They can be found in many theological orientations, every educational endeavor, and in all parts of the world.

Today New Age thought appears in the following areas:

1. Many training seminars offering self-improvement contain New Age thought. In some cases it is implicit rather

than explicit. Exercises such as biofeedback, meditation, centering, visualization, gaming, and simulation may appear harmless. In reality, they may be channels for New Age thought.

Many practitioners, unless they are Christians, believe in the holistic interrelatedness of all things. Religious expressions of New Age thought include a belief in *panentheism.* This is the belief that God is in all things. It is distinguished from *pantheism,* which believes that God is all things. Pantheism holds that God is not a personality. All the laws, forces, and powers of the universe are God. Panentheism does not hold that all things are God, only that in all things, God is present. This may appear on the surface to be "much ado about nothing." In truth, there is a subtle difference.

The problem with this is evident: if God is in all things, how can there be any sin, since God and sin are incompatible? If panentheism is true, evil cannot exist. In addition, adherence to panentheism results in the loss of a personal God, one who has personality and all the characteristics of personality. This creates a problem for any meaningful communication with God. How can one communicate with a God who has no personality but somehow consists essentially in everything?

New Age thought preaches about the God who is within us all. Each one is endowed with divinity. This is not the same as saying each one is God. New Age thought points humankind to the inner divinity, and this is why it is so important to get in touch with oneself. Meditation and visualization become means of grace for New Age worshipers.

If God dwells in every person, then there was no need for Jesus' death on the Cross. His reconciling death was for nothing, since God is already in all humankind. This idea clearly differs from Paul's description of the "God [who] was in Christ, reconciling the world unto himself" (2 Cor.

5:19). The New Testament paints a picture of a loving God, grieved over the lostness of His creation, seeking, searching, and working for their rescue. Accordingly, the New Testament describes humanity as estranged from God. God is not in their hearts, else God would not have to initiate a mighty rescue effort.

Jesus tells of the searching shepherd looking for the lost lamb. It is a description of His ministry on earth. It defines the very character of God. If God was already in the hearts of humankind, there would be no reason for Jesus the Son to come to earth.

Some have made Jesus' words, "The kingdom of God is within you" (Luke 17:21), a proof-text to support the idea of divinity within. Biblical scholars remind us that this text can just as easily be translated, "The kingdom of God is among you" (KJV margin). The most obvious conclusion is that Jesus came to bring the kingdom of God to every heart. Upon our faith, trust, and acceptance of the Lord Jesus Christ, the kingdom of God is placed in our hearts.

2. Creativity training is often a fertile ground for New Age thought. While creativity training can be morally neutral, it often contains the belief that divinity resides in every person in a way quite different from the Christian belief of the image of God in man. Becoming creative, according to New Age thought, means releasing yourself from whatever hindrances might exist. Such release might involve divorce from one's partner, leaving one's religion, or adopting practices that clearly do not conform to God's Word.

Christians do not deny the untapped potential that lies dormant in many individuals. Christians believe in those actions that can be taken to release and encourage higher levels of performance.

The problem with much New Age creativity training is the underlying philosophical message it conveys. To encourage achievement and performance is a worthy goal. To insist, however, that humans are capable of increased performance because divinity resides within them is erroneous. To encourage visualization of skill-based performance is morally neutral. To visualize some inner power being released that somehow transforms the individual can be dangerous.

The danger that is involved is subtle. Opening one's mind to the idea that there are forces and powers waiting to be tapped to help one achieve performance beyond the ordinary may sound innocent. Scripture reminds us that there are spiritual powers working in the world that we clearly do not understand (Eph. 2:2). One popular writer has referred to the power of the "ascended Masters."[6] One must not confuse these so-called ascended masters with the power God can unleash through His Holy Spirit in the individual believer. The origins of these so-called ascended masters is certainly not biblical.

Creativity training is not rejected out of hand by Christians. It is important, however, that believers be fully informed of the philosophical base on which any training of this type rests.

3. Popular self-help books offer a wide variety of "cures," many of which are based on the fundamental principle of New Age thought: God is within you, you are divine, you can solve your own problems. No dream is beyond your reach. No obstacle need hinder you. Such books cover a wide territory, as New Age thought is elastic enough to provide room for everyone.

Our world is intensely competitive. As environments and economies change, personal performance becomes more critical in terms of employment, advancement, and success. Earthly systems ordering everyday life deliver stresses and strains upon the fragile self-image we all possess. When our competitiveness as significant players is questioned, we look for the quick fix. We cannot afford to miss the promotions that ensure college tuition for our children or security for retirement years. When the fine balance of economic or social equilibrium is endangered, many of us turn to the popular self-help literature of the day.

Perhaps New Age thought has never been so attractively packaged as it has been in the popular self-help section of our bookstores. As Christians, we would never think of purchasing a book boldly declaring self-help through New Age ideas. We are, however, without knowing, often exposed to the central themes of this system in these kinds of books. This illustrates the subtlety of the whole movement. All too often, we have associated New Age thought with the outrageous, outlandish, and ridiculous. Yet the subtle presentation of these views in harmless-looking books is one of the most dangerous areas of this philosophy's penetration into our culture.

4. Stress management programs may unconsciously involve one in New Age thought. The essential activities of many stress management programs involve getting in touch with one's feelings. While there are many legitimate programs that stimulate constructive approaches to stress management, be sure to "read the fine print" if you participate. Getting in touch with one's feelings without acknowledging the state of one's relationship to God can be counterproductive.

Such ideas are counter to the truths put forward in God's Word. Nowhere in Scripture are Christians counseled to get in touch with their feelings. To be sure, feelings are important. True Christian religion affects the emotions and feelings. Our feelings, however, are unreliable guides and are never of themselves sufficient sources of spiritual growth.

Christians can and do experience stress and its related consequences. There may even be times when professional counselors may suggest remedies involving the emotions, their expression, and their management. For the believer, Jesus is Lord of life. He is our temporal Lord, which means

He is Lord of our times, and He is our spiritual Lord. His Lordship is not something tied only to our religious rituals or observances.

In Matthew Jesus is called Emmanuel, which means "God [is] with us" (1:23). Getting in touch with the living presence of Christ provides more in the way of stress management strategies than any New Age-derived program. Feelings and emotions are valuable elements of the human experience. It is Jesus Christ who can transform those emotions into working elements that enrich rather than imperil human life. Scripture reminds us that Jesus brings joy, peace, and contentment to life. Far from inhibiting true feelings and emotions, Jesus releases our emotions from the crippling impairments of self-centeredness.

New Age thought is attractive, especially to those who are looking for secular answers to the riddles and problems of life. It offers an appealing idea: "You can work your own miracles."[7] The power for these miracles is not to be found in some external religious experience, but within you. Divinity resides within you, and you can tap that unlimited power on command.

The Christian must ever be alert to the subtle dangers posed by New Age thought. In the next section, we will learn how to recognize this mentality.

2

How to Recognize New Age Thought

It was one of those crisp, sunny, New England mornings that you can almost feel when you're looking at the cover of a scenic American calendar. I left my hotel to walk several blocks to the main street of West Hartford, Conn. I stepped inside a café to eat breakfast before the first session of the day. I was there to learn how to keep new people in our churches once we get them to attend.

A young, bearded Anglican priest from Canada asked if he could join me as I ate. Interested in what he might have to say, I invited him to sit down.

Because he was wearing the collar of the clergy, my preconceived notions prevented me from being prepared for what he was about to say. He started by telling me how much he resented New Age thought being bootlegged into the training sessions. All ears, I asked him to go on.

"Take, for instance, those biofeedback dots we all wore yesterday. This is another example of how the seminar leader is mingling New Age thought with the claims of the gospel. It just won't work. You can't put New Age thought and the gospel together."

I thought about the bio dots of the previous day. True enough, we did wear them. The instructor told us to monitor the color of the dots. Black or dark brown indicated that we were tense, even anxious. Light blue, on the other hand, indicated relaxation and readiness to learn.

I looked down at mine, and sure enough, it was dark brown.

Now I'm a fairly relaxed person. I'm not usually nervous, tense, or anxious. Getting my dot to change colors seemed to be a simple assignment.

The instructor said to clear our minds of clutter. Focus on calming thoughts. So I began to pray silently.

No change. Maybe it turned a little yellow, but no big change. I looked over at a Unitarian pastor, and his dot had changed to sky blue. I thought, I wonder what he's doing to make that dot change colors.

The instructor gave us time to meditate and reflect. By now, I was getting a little nervous. Only moments ago, I had walked through the crisp New England sunshine. I had listened to the birds on the village green. I had marveled at the tall trees surrounding the beautiful church in which the seminar was being conducted. I had just concluded a time of prayer and felt the inner assurance of the Spirit that all was in right relationship between me and the Savior.

My dot, however, wouldn't cooperate. It was still in the color range indicating I wasn't relaxed. By now I was convinced that my dot was defective. Why didn't it change color? I even repeated Peter's admonition, "Casting all your care upon him; for he careth for you" (1 Pet. 5:7).

The instructor asked volunteers to share from their experience with the class. The Unitarian preacher went first.

He told us how he has made meditation a regular part of his day; that he has learned much from transcendental meditation, yoga, and native peoples' spirituality. He told how his experiences in these areas helped him tremendously as he was going through his divorce. And that it has helped his church grow, and that they in turn had helped him transform his divorce into a personal growth experience.

My breakfast companion, the Anglican priest, continued.

"My parish is a small one in southeastern Ontario. We have been through all this meditation and New Age stuff. It left us cold. Then one day one of my members began telling me about an experience with the Holy Spirit. I didn't think much of it," he said.

"As I began to study and listen to the Word, I knew this was what I needed. Today, God is moving in my parish. He is healing people, putting broken families together, and we are growing again."

As my experience in the class demonstrated, if there is one word to describe the infiltration of New Age thought, it is the word, *pervasive*. New Age influence has literally spread throughout our culture and society. There is no field of endeavor untouched by its influence, from theology to corporate training. New Age ideas appear in the literature we read, the television programs we watch, and the popular ideas we hear discussed. The word *pervasive* comes from the root word *pervade*, which means "to pass through, to be diffused throughout."[1]

Not long ago, employees of Pacific Telesis went to court over New Age infiltration in corporate training programs. One popular newsmagazine called it "guru mind control."

Professional associations charged with the responsibility for setting standards for consulting firms have taken interest in the frequency of complaints. Complaints have come from participants in corporate training programs over the frequent appearance of New Age thought.

If we are to be alert Christians, we need to know where and what to look for.

For What Do We Look?

New Age thought often appeals to people who value innovation. These are the people who enjoy change. They are attracted by the introduction of any new idea, method, or concept. They are often the people who are on the cutting edge. They are dissatisfied with traditional ideas. They want to know where the action is, where the late-breaking ideas are. For many people, traditional approaches just don't cut it anymore. They are tired of the threadbare clichés and the usual answers. When New Age thought comes along, they are quick to transfer their allegiance.

There is nothing inherently wrong with innovation. The world is full of valuable things directly resulting from someone's creativity. For the Christian, innovation has limits, especially on matters to which the Bible speaks clearly and directly. In the world of invention, design, communication, and discovery, Christians freely use divergent strategies to achieve breakthroughs.

In the spiritual realm, believers live within the boundaries established by a loving God. Innovation, i.e., the introduction of new ideas, is a welcome strategy regarding our methods. The message by which we live, however, remains off-limits to the tampering of would-be innovators.

New Age thought is innovative. It values *celebration, dialogue with Eastern religions,* and *native religions.* It blends materials from the human potential movement, the new physics, and the environmental groups. In addition, it has a strong focus on *getting in touch with your feelings.*

Many studying New Age thought for the first time are puzzled by the terms and descriptions used to define both its message and its variety. Let's look at the terms in that last paragraph for a moment.

When we say New Age thought values *celebration,* are we implying that traditional thought does not? No. New Age thought values the earthiness of humankind and therefore celebrates nature and what is natural about human existence. This celebration is not to be confused with praise. Christians praise their Creator-God as His creatures, and His gift of creation. New Age thought celebrates nature and the natural order. These two extremes may be thought of in terms of a simple diagram:

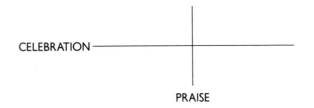

CELEBRATION

PRAISE

Celebration is horizontal, involving like beings, while praise is vertical, involving the praiser with a higher being.

New Age thought is oriented to a worldview that is conditioned by evolutionary belief. Traditional Christian thought historically believed in a divine creation totally consistent with the Genesis account. Presently, some Christian thinkers are comfortable with a modified evolutionary position. They accept the legitimate findings of science as possible answers to the riddle of origins. They believe, however, that the Ultimate Cause of all existence is God.

New Age thought attempts to link modern life, with all its knowledge and technology, to the earthiness of humankind's less technological, more natural existence. Celebration for New Age thinkers is the link between these extremes. A present example is the New Age idea of goddess worship.

Goddess worship includes fertility rites, a belief in a harmonious world, and the importance of the female "energies," e.g., intuition, nurturing, and compassion.[2] According to Judith D. Auerbach, of University of Southern California's Institute for the Study of Women and Men: "Goddess worshippers believe that to recreate a harmonious world, traits they consider male (dominance, aggressiveness, competitiveness) must give way to female 'energies.' "[3]

Goddess worship centers around the celebration of these "energies," calling for harmony among all living things. There are goddess books, newsletters, cable TV shows, and a goddess hotline. Goddess worship is springing up from one coast to the other.

New Age thought is often compared with traditional Eastern religions. In fact, many of the beliefs of Hinduism and Buddhism appear in New Age thought. Perhaps the most frequently mentioned belief is reincarnation. Native peoples' religions, often called spiritualities, are highly valued in New Age thought. This includes the religions of the American Indians, some African beliefs, and the traditional belief in witchcraft.

One of the strengths of New Age thought is its flexibility. One does not necessarily have to buy into witchcraft to participate in the new thinking. One's experience in this adventure can be as complex as goddess worship or as simple as just getting in touch with your feelings. It is important to understand that New Age thought is a spectrum, i.e., a long line that extends well across the horizon. You will find infinite variety along that line.

One characteristic that draws people to New Age thought is its novelty. Many people are turned off by tradition. They are looking for the newest ideas the state-of-the-art approach. New Age ideas provide many different forms of human expression to explore as methods of spirituality. For example, one may use art, dance, clay modeling, or gardening, to name a few of the meditation forms.

A word that is commonly used in New Age thought is *spirituality*. Since so much of their agenda is rarely labeled "New Age," one should listen carefully whenever the term *spirituality* is used. It is one of those terms whose meaning has been exchanged for another. To the traditional Christian, it has reference to the life of the Spirit, implying the power and presence of the Holy Spirit.

In New Age tradition, spirituality refers to whatever influence, content, or practice is currently being used to experience life at a level other than the purely intellectual. It is at this point that New Age thought borrows most heavily from traditional spiritualism. Put aside the familiar understanding that spiritualists are only those who claim contact with the dead. Think instead of the formal understanding of spiritualism, which holds that all reality is in essence spiritual.

With this understanding, one can see how New Age practices include such diverse elements as dance, art, clay modeling, gardening, and many others. For many New Agers, any practice that puts them in touch with their feelings, their earthiness, is legitimate, because all existence or reality is essentially spiritual. It is also clear why meditation and visualization are so important. The reality one experiences through meditative or visualization practices is just as "real" as is present physical reality.

With this in view, it is clear why much confusion exists surrounding the New Age movement, particularly as it crosses over into the realm of traditional theology and religion. The beliefs of Christians and New Agers intersect at many critical points. Christians believe in spiritual existence. They know that "faith is the substance of things hoped for, the evidence of things not seen" (Heb. 11:1). By the same token, New Agers also believe in the world they cannot see. They, too, believe in the reality of things unseen.

The difference between Christians and New Agers, whether they are in traditional churches or not, is significant. Christians believe the way to God is only through Jesus Christ. For the New Ager, the way to spirituality is through many different paths and practices. When Christians and New Agers speak of spiritualities, they are not speaking of the same things.

One of the fundamentals of New Age thought is the idea that divinity is not something external to humankind. It is internal and intrinsic to all.

If there is a "fundamentalism" in religious New Age thought, it would be this:

1. Deny the idea of an angry God who is upset over your sin.

2. Look beyond the Cross to a vision of the god who is within you.

3. Reject the notions of a demanding God with absolute laws. A spiritual hierarchy or concepts of right and wrong, good and evil, are all remnants of the dualism that must be avoided.

4. Replace traditional religious thinking with insights from the collective wisdom of humanity, the unity of nature, our unity with the environment, and other human beings.

New Age thought steps into the vacuum created by the sterility of technology. The last third of the 20th century has brought changes that seem to overwhelm the strongest among us. The institutions so familiar to us appear in danger of crumbling or collapsing altogether. We feel disconnected from our roots. Into this world of confusion, two or three powerful forces have been unleashed:

1. The primitive force attempting to capture technology like Attila the Hun captured Rome. Spend some time watching popular rock videos on cable television, and you will see a bizarre combination of primal primitiveness and contemporary technology.

2. The "mad scientist" phenomenon at work that suggests science can solve all problems. Of course with every "solution" comes unforeseen and unwanted side effects demanding another "solution."

3. The New Age phenomena that suggest that humankind's hope lies in the construction of an alternative reality, one that balances technology with respect for the environment and all living creatures.

The resulting confusion has taken much of mainline Christianity captive. At the close of the 19th century, mainline Protestant churches were busy unloading their belief in miracles, the divinity of Jesus Christ, His virgin birth, a literal resurrection, and much more. The Bible was reduced to a sourcebook of *descriptive, inspirational sources* useful in creating one's own story. The result reduced that wing of Christianity to just another among many competing ethical systems, useful in helping people put higher ideals in their lives.

This bankruptcy was noticed by some as the number of members and converts started to decline. Mainline Christian churches began hemorrhaging at alarming rates. Many stopgap measures were tried. Social activism appeared in the 1960s. Ecumenism was tried but failed. New Age ideas were given new terms or names and imported. Still the hemorrhaging continued.

Today there are more Muslims in the U.S.A. than Episcopalians. Wade Clark Roof writes: "Hundreds of religious and spiritual groups new to the American scene have emerged: Eastern mystical faiths, with an emphasis on meditation and reincarnation as well as groups drawing upon a wide assortment of older, more primitive traditions re-cast in new form, such as nature religions, Native American practices, theosophical beliefs, goddess worship and other New Age spiritualities."[4]

New Age thought understands the emptiness of modern humankind cut adrift from the life-giving source of spiritual relationships. It understands the harsh, cold, winter night of the spirit, living only with the toys of technology. By emphasizing the harmony of all living things, the value of celebration, and the importance of spiritual existence, New Age thought is making a strong appeal. To those who found traditional Christian religion stripped of its power and robbed of its feeling, New Age thought is an appealing substitute.

New Age thought also understands the loneliness of the spirit that is the result of pain and separation. Our world is full of individuals whose daily lives are full of more pain than most of us can imagine. Just getting through another day is a big task for some. They are alone, with small children to raise, or they are cut off from a support system that could sustain them. Their lives are full of the quiet loneliness that shouts in terrifying stillness. For whatever reason or circumstance, they remain isolated from the warmth of traditional religious communities of faith. Perhaps they have experienced rejection and cannot tolerate another such experience. For them New Age thought may offer an attractive alternative.

New Age groups speak of *synergy.* The definition of this term comes from the root word *synergism.* As terms go, it is neutral. Defined, it means the simultaneous action of separate elements, working together to produce a greater total effect than either of the elements working alone. Those involved in New Age groups believe they are contributing to each other, and from their joint contributions they will become more than they could be alone. As they meditate, exercise, work, visualize, or just fellowship together, they believe they are tapping spiritual realities that combine to make them more than they were. In this case, synergy is related to the New Age concept of holism.

In New Age terminology, there is abundant use of words containing multiple meanings. One such word is *holism.* Whereas Christians use the term to illustrate harmonious relationships between the parts making up the whole, New Agers refer to interconnection between spirit, matter, and energy. This harmonious interconnection can be experienced through meditation and visualization, and the understanding that all reality is essentially spiritual.

To summarize, we can say according to New Age thought:

1. Sin does not exist.

2. There is only the failure to be connected with the cosmos in compassionate, caring, and creative ways.

3. There is no holiness, only holism.

4. There are no absolutes, only pointers drawn from many sources.

The four foundational themes that lie at the heart of New Age spirituality are these:

1. Global interdependence

2. Mystery, mysticism, awe, and reverence for whatever is not understood in the ordinary physical or material sense

3. Personal experience

4. Transformation

Where Do We Look?

Practitioners using New Age influences may or may not be aware of their presence. It is important that we be skilled in evaluating our experiences. We must be able to discern error and react according to our Christian conscience. If you are biblically illiterate, you may fall into a New Age trap without knowing it. Here are just several of many critical areas to watch for the presence of New Age-derived thought:

1. Training seminars designed around personal improvement strategies

2. Stress management seminars

3. Creativity training

4. Popular self-help materials

5. Nontraditional learning techniques

6. Corporate management training programs

Many training programs and seminars use the following:

1. Biofeedback
2. Meditation
3. Centering
4. Visualization and imaging
5. Gaming
6. Simulation

While these may appear benign or harmless on the surface, they are nonetheless open-ended opportunities for practitioners to bootleg New Age thought. These practices can become the vehicles in which the new beliefs can be transported. Usually practitioners using these, unless born again through the blood of Jesus Christ, believe the following:

1. A belief in holism that suggests the interrelatedness of all things. Religious expression of New Age thought includes belief in panentheism. This is the belief that God is in all things, that there is nothing in which God is not in. The holism of the New Ager is not to be confused with the holism of the therapist. The therapist may speak of holism as it harmoniously relates all working parts to the whole. The belief in panentheism is inseparably related to the New Age idea of holism.

   a. The problem Christians have with such thinking is clear: If God is in all things, how can sin possibly exist?

   b. This is a direct contradiction of God's Word. Jesus said, "In my Father's house," referring to the dwelling place of God. He said, "I go to the Father" (John 14:2 and 16:16).

   c. If God dwells automatically in every person, then there was no need for Jesus' death on the Cross. Calvary was all for nothing.

2. They believe that humanity does not need an external Savior. They believe in the essential, native goodness of humanity. They discount the notion of original sin. Since there can't be original sin, what is the need for a Savior?

　　a. How else can we explain humankind's capacity for incredibly evil behavior, unless, of course, we recognize the presence of sin in the human heart? Scripture confirms this (see Jer. 17:9; Matt. 15:19).

3. They believe that dualism is an intolerable belief. According to New Age thought, dualism divides, while holism heals and reconciles. Some examples of the dualisms discouraged by New Age thinkers are these:

　　a. Male/female

　　b. Me/you

　　c. Black/white

The problem Christians have with this criticism is based on the fact that Jesus used such categories to identify the spiritual condition of humanity. He spoke of the wise and the unwise, the sheep and the goats, the foolish builder and the wise builder.

4. They believe in the "christ spirit" rather than in the Christ of the Bible. The litmus test of any theology, religion, or philosophy is its viewpoint concerning the divinity of Jesus Christ, the Son of God. The idea of the "christ spirit" is one that frequently appears in traditional Hinduism. George Harrison, former Beatle, sings this in his song "My Sweet Lord" when he sings identical praises to "Krishna." He is actually singing of Lord Krishna, the "christ spirit."

New Age thinking is probably nowhere as blatant as it is in some forms of creativity training. Consider this from David H. Lyman's article "Being Creative":

"Can we teach them creativity? No, but we can help them rediscover what it is to be creative.

"Our task is to help them unlearn the things that keep them from being creative. Our job is to tell them it's all right to let go, to be disorganized, spontaneous, even spiritual."[5]

You may think, "That doesn't sound too bad." Perhaps when you hear Lyman's description of creative people and the steps one should take to become creative, you may change your mind.

Lyman's List of Creative Traits:

1. They are different.
2. They are playful.
3. They do not play by the rules.
4. They are adventurous.
5. They have trouble being accurate, punctual, and proper.

And many more . . .

Lyman says, "We all have the power to become who we want to become. The trouble is, we often pick up the wrong script . . .

"It has been my experience that people who are well behaved, agreeable, accommodating, and cooperative are seldom creative." Creative people "drive their families crazy" with their "selfish attention, unpredictableness, inconsiderateness, arrogance, cantankerousness, irreverence, and their failure to take other people seriously."[6]

Clearly, this is New Age material. This type of thought abhors the straitjacket of conventional wisdom and philosophy. This stems from the inherent idea that we are not judgment-bound individuals who will someday be called into account for our actions. Our actions, they declare, must not be restricted by a dead moralism that depends on some code written in history's dim light, thousands of years ago. To truly become creative, one must "let go." This usually means forsaking the restraints of traditional philosophy, whether it is derived from biblical religion or the wisdom of one's elders. In any case such restraints are not in keeping with the reality of the divinity that resides within one.

Compare that with the following scripture:

"This know also, that in the last days perilous times shall come. For men shall be lovers of their own selves, covetous, boasters, proud, blasphemers, disobedient to parents, unthankful, unholy, without natural affection, truce-breakers, false accusers, incontinent, fierce, despisers of those that are good, traitors, heady, highminded, lovers of pleasures more than lovers of God; having a form of godliness, but denying the power thereof: from such turn away" (2 Tim. 3:1-5).

To summarize, it is important that Christians be able to recognize the philosophy that underlies New Age thought. Rarely, if ever, will you read or see the words "New Age." Because of the craziness associated with some of New Age's proponents like Guru MA, Shirley MacLaine, JZ Knight, and a host of others, the very term has become somewhat discredited.

It is important that we believers know how to discern truth from falsehood. It is important that we know how to evaluate life's experiences from a biblical understanding. It is important that we read, study, and internalize God's Word.

But there is another important reason for developing our Christian powers of discernment and discrimination.

When one opens one's mind to guided meditation, visualization, or imaging techniques, you are at the mercies of that individual. If you allow one who is not filled with the Spirit of Christ to have access to your mind, you may open the door for the inrush of the very demons of hell.

We must be careful not to disregard the warnings of Jesus in this regard if we expect to walk in fellowship with Him. Remember the "hard saying of Jesus":

"And if thy right eye offend thee, pluck it out, and cast it from thee: for it is profitable for thee that one of thy members should perish, and not that thy whole body should be cast into hell. And if thy right hand offend thee, cut it off, and cast it from thee: for it is profitable for thee that one of thy members should perish, and not that thy whole body should be cast into hell" (Matt. 5:29-30).

If what you are thinking about, what you're doing, or where you're going is endangering your soul, it is better to stop thinking about it, stop doing it, and stop going there, in order to escape Christ's condemnation.

In order to communicate the serious threat New Age thought contains, we must learn how to recognize error. Instead of using angry accusation and blasting rhetoric to combat this power, let us instruct others how to avoid the pitfalls. As we walk in fellowship with the Savior, we can depend on His guidance. United to Jesus, we cannot fall.

3

The Heart of New Age Thought

In the Bible, we learn that God is both "here" as well as "there." This is one of those paradoxes that is difficult for us to understand. We are limited by space and time to being in one place at one time. God is not bound by such limitations. As a result, we can speak of God present in our midst, as well as the One who inhabits eternity.

Theologians thoughtfully study Scripture with the idea of helping us understand more completely the complexity of Divinity as it relates to the human condition. One result of their studies is the development of theological language, or terms that more precisely convey the meanings of their findings.

Two theological terms that are important to our understanding of New Age thought are *immanence* and *transcendence*. Christians believe that God is both immanent, i.e., here and present with us through the Holy Spirit, as well as transcendent, i.e., beyond us. If we emphasize one concept at the expense of the other, our theology becomes deformed. When our theology is wrong, our practices are affected. Since practice and behavior follow theology, wrong theology can produce wrong living and wrong worship.

New Age thought emphasizes the immanence of God at the expense of His transcendence. In other words, this system believes God dwells in every person, every being, every life-form. Of course, it is not the God of the Bible that dwells there. It is a mysterious god, a life-force, a creative energy that dwells there. It is not the personal God of the Bible that is familiar to all Christians.

For some who profess faith in the Christian religion, this New Age emphasis upon immanence is a welcome idea. To speak of a God who inhabits all of time, space, and eternity is to speak of One whose greatness is beyond comprehension. Mortal beings like men and women, created in His image, stand as inferior beings before Him. They owe Him their worship, their service, their submission. This is the idea of the transcendent God. To those uncomfortable with such a view, an immanent God who somehow exists just below the surface of every being is much more comforting. Immanence emphasized at the expense of transcendence reduces the need for our reconciliation to God. What need is there to be reconciled to Him when He is already present just below the surface of my life?

New Age thought has infiltrated some expressions of Christian thought at this point. The New Ager speaks of getting in touch with his feelings. Why? Because at that level there is the potential of being in contact with the divinity that resides within us all. The truth is, this is not new in the sense that is just now appearing on the horizon of religious thought. It is quite old.

Some who have written or spoken about New Age thought have believed it necessary to specifically identify organizations or proponents with the label "New Age." Without doubt, there are dangers that need to be avoided and perhaps even organizations, books, materials, etc., of which to be wary. What is far more critical to me is for believers to develop the skills they need for understanding the differences between truth and error. Recognition of error is the first step in avoiding it. Error is not always easy to detect. Most of the time, error is best represented by a different shading, that is, it is a clever mixture of truth and falsehood.

New Age thought emphasizes the group over the individual. While it is true that its leaders preach a divinity residing in each person, the larger emphasis is on unification rather than individualization.

Earlier in this work, the idea of all existence being essentially some form of energy was mentioned. This is often associated with the findings of the new physics. To briefly review, the older physics held that the universe consisted of matter and energy, or some combination of the two. The new physics holds the unification of all existence. Existence is equated with energy.

These ideas are not new in the sense that they are making their appearance for the first time. In the 1860s, Mary Baker Eddy founded Christian Science with similar ideas. She believed that the universe consisted of the Divine Mind. By prayer and faith, believers could tap the Divine Mind for their benefit. Other examples of this theory may be found by the student of religion. What held them in common was their belief in the presence of Universal Mind or Oversoul. This Universal Mind existed in each individual, according to them, as a spark exists in relationship to a fire.

New Age thought has captured this old idea and given it new and varied expressions, depending on the source one reads or studies. This is one reason for the movement's emphasis on holism and synergy.[1]

New Age thought has no room for the individual standing alone before God to be judged for his life. Ideas that speak of individual responsibility and duty are replaced with group relationships. *Networking* is a buzzword for many of their groups. It indicates the belief in the interconnectedness and unity of all things.

New Age-influenced Christianity feels at home with this emphasis on unity as opposed to individualism. Some

New Age Christian thinkers speak of the danger of "privatization" of religious experience. This is the concern that the individual will become so absorbed in his relationship with God that it will subordinate his relationship to the wider society. Privatization of religious experience, they contend, leads to an emphasis on personalism. Personalism is the belief that God is personal and that He is to be worshiped personally by the individual. Such thinkers caution against speaking of one's "personal salvation" or of Jesus as one's "personal Savior."

Christianity has always balanced the value of the individual with the importance of the group. Perhaps no greater network has ever existed in the world than the Christian Church. Biblical Christianity urges both the belief and practice of life in the Christian Body. The chief difference rests in the fact that Jesus Christ is the Central Figure around which the Church, His Body, revolves. Christians face a creative irony: they act both as individual believers and as the collective Church. This tension, however, is carefully balanced by the fact that God is both present with us in the form of His Holy Spirit, and that He is beyond us, calling us ever forward toward Him.

When the believer comes before God at the Final Judgment, he will not stand as the representative of the Church, but as an individual, created in the image of God, and redeemed by the blood of Jesus, God's Son.

New Age thought does not buy the idea of Christ's uniqueness. As long as Christians speak of Jesus the teacher, the new group has little difficulty with Him. It is when Christians claim divinity for Jesus that New Agers break with them.

New Age thought opens its arms to Hindus, Buddhists, secularists, atheists, and even witches. Native peoples' religions are held on a par with the Christian religion. As long as all parties are talking about the "christ spirit," the term "christ" can be used without difficulty. To them, the "christ spirit" is the "hero," the "suffering servant," the "mystical one." It is important that Christians have their terms defined according to the norms of Scripture when talking with those involved in this thought.

This new movement is home to many traditions. Let's take a look at who's coming to dinner:

1. Hindus such as Maharishi Mahesh Yogi, who believe in the Unified Field Theory.[2] This is the belief the universe consists of only energy. This energy is subdivided into seven states of consciousness.

2. Those who believe that the universe is made up of Universal Mind.

3. Those who believe in creation spiritualities, e.g., Matthew Fox.[3]

4. Those who believe in Mother Earth, the so-called "green spiritualities," the environmentalists.[4]

The Christian religion recognizes the importance of environmental protection and the understanding of global interdependence. The difference between Christians and New Agers is our total reliance upon Jesus Christ for our salvation. There is no other salvation. To speak of a unified universe, an intelligence that provides a common spark in every person, is incomplete without discussion about God, His creation, its fall into sin, and the great rescue operation effected by God's Son, Jesus Christ.

New Age thought categorically rejects absolutes. It believes in relativism. This is the understanding that no absolutes exist in the sense that humankind are bound by them. Of course this is nothing new. The problems with this position are very clear. Without absolutes, life has no fixed center, no point of reference. Without a reference point, a compass is useless. Without a compass there is no way to determine the direction of the course.

If society were to adopt such a view, all systems of justice would break down. Instead of being guarded by legal certainties, society would be at the mercies of the amoral.

Existence would soon degenerate into a baffling setting of situational ethics. In other words, the situation would define the ethics.

This is a serious problem for Western civilization. Values clarification exercises can consist of recognizing all points of view as valid; none are either right or wrong, only expedient or not expedient. Our culture is being swept by a pluralism that demands not only a hearing for every position but protection under the law as well.

For Christians, salvation by grace through faith is the crowning experience of the human condition. For New Agers, it is self-realization.

We must realize that New Age thought did not arrive on the scene in full form. It is founded on a variety of previous philosophical foundations expressed over time. It has a "Velcro philosophy," i.e., it captures bits and pieces from a wide variety of philosophical sources.

Self-realization, or as Maslow suggested, self-actualization, may have been a respectable term in the literature of legitimate psychology. Under the New Age umbrella it may mean many different things to many different people. It has even been suggested that Jesus Christ, along with a select few others, was among the very few that ever achieved self-actualization.

Today, self-actualization has become self-realization. If one desires to express himself in a particular way, that is his undeniable right. The right of self-realization through self-expression is highly valued in New Age thought.

Christians believe that human beings exist as they do only through the permissive will of God. We know that humankind's greatest need is a Savior with the power to forgive, redeem, and restore. New Agers insist that all the power one needs to effect personal transformation resides within. Believers know that such promises can never be kept.

It comes down to this: Christians want to achieve their personal best, but they know it can't be done without a Savior. That Savior is Jesus Christ.

New Age thought sees a primary relationship between humans and their natural environment. Nature is important in much of this thinking. As a result, mysticism, mystery, and awe are important concepts. For people living in the noise, pollution, and hustle of civilization, any appeal to what is natural looks good. And many individuals have been turned off by sterile, cold, and formal worship services in Christian churches. They listen to a provocative beat in their daily music. They are bombarded with advertising that challenges them to let go and live it up. Letting go, having fun, and being free seems natural to them.

New Age thought emphasizes what Christians would call the "creation" at the expense of the Creator. Christians stand in relation to the Creator who created them precisely for their environment. Creation is not evil. It has been invaded by evil, and therefore it is tarnished or marred. Because of this, some misguided Christians associated matter, or physical creation, with evil. With this association came a "don't touch" mentality. This was followed with all sorts of rules and regulations to prevent future believers from being contaminated through their contact with the world.

New Agers often see Christians as "fun-less" people, living containerized lives, cut off from creation. Nothing could be further from the truth. It is by standing in relationship to the Creator that the Christian most fully appreciates creation. Any attempt to explain creation from perspectives other than a relationship with the Creator reduce creation to an ugly swamp. It becomes a swamp in which the whirlpools of pornography, perversion, and self-destruction abound.

By the same token, creation cannot serve as a resource in our attempts to understand humankind's ultimate purpose. If we generalize, as New Age thought does, from our observations of nature to the duties and responsibilities of humankind, we will inevitably draw false conclusions. If we appeal to examples found in creation without taking into consideration the damage done to it by the invasion of sin, we will err.

Cain well remembered the stories his father, Adam, told him of the Garden of Eden. No doubt he listened intently as Adam told him of the communion he and Cain's mother, Eve, had nightly with God. Cain understood the fact that he and his family were estranged from Him. He knew that his parents were clothed with the skins of animals God had slain. He must have grasped, even if only remotely, that the disobedience of his parents was atoned by the shedding of blood.

When the time came for him to worship God, instead of offering the blood taken from an animal He had created, Cain offered the produce of the fields of his own cultivation. Instead of following the directives laid down by God, Cain tried to reason out his own approach. God did not accept Cain's offering.

New Age thought repeats the mistake of Cain. It is a clever attempt to reason out a solution to the problems brought about by humankind's alienation from God. Just as Cain's offering was bloodless, New Age thought offers a promise without persecution. It offers a solution without a Savior. It trumpets a spirituality without godliness.

New Age thought is riddled with half-truths, near truths, and outright lies. Only the pure, unadulterated truth of God's Word can make us free to live the abundant life. Jesus is the Way, the Truth, and the Life (see John 14:6).

4

Evangelizing Those in New Age Thought

I had known Steven since he was about four years old. I wasn't close to him. But I knew him, and he remembered me.

It had been years since I last saw him. Then, he was a little boy, playing with my sons and their cousins in southern California. Rumor was that Steven's mother was a perpetual drug abuser who was in and out of clinics, rehab centers, and detox facilities.

Steven was a poor little rich boy. His mother was the daughter of a wealthy southern California family. She was a child of the '60s and somewhere along the line got lost in the haze of Haight-Ashbury in San Francisco and 1,000 other would-be nirvanas.

I lost touch with Steven. Frankly, the only time I thought of him was during those times when we talked about his mother and the tragedy of her life.

The years of my life sped by. Then one day at a central California motel, I stood face-to-face with Steven. What I saw was incredible. No longer the little skinny boy that played with my sons, he wore no shirt, no shoes, a red goatee, and the most fantastic tattoos I had ever seen.

Like something out of a Music Television nightmare, Steven's body was covered from neckline to the top of his bare feet with gruesome, bizarre, and revolting body art in the form of tattoos.

I politely nodded a stiff "hello" when told that this was Steven. When asked if I remembered him, I tried to dismiss the image of the present, looking for the memories of our past acquaintance.

Our families were together for a wedding. In the hustle and bustle, I saw little of Steven as he was either off alone on his own or with other young men.

On the day of the wedding, Steven waited until the last minute to dress. My wife and family and I went on to be seated at the church. As the prelude was being performed, I looked up to see an usher seat Steven by my side. I turned, looked into his eyes, only to realize why he had waited to dress. Steven was off in the fog of what polite society calls "substance abuse."

The wedding went as weddings do, and soon we were outside to greet the bride and groom. The rice was thrown, and the couple left. Who was standing there, by my side, but Steven. I summoned my courage to speak to him about his soul. I knew that I had an obligation, but more than that, I had an opportunity. I would either take it now or maybe lose it and never see Steven this side of eternity.

I asked Steven if he ever gave his spiritual development much thought. He replied that he did, and that he had been reading the Bible. He said, "You know, I only read the words in red. I like Jesus, but I don't like the other stuff too much."

I heard my next cue. I said, "Steven, tell me what you think of Jesus."

He told me of his interest and his admiration for Jesus the Man.

I asked him if he understood that Jesus claimed to be more than just a man, that He claimed to be the Son of God. We talked about the familiar detours; his dislike of the church and institutionalized religion. I kept pointing him to Jesus who loved him and gave His life for him.

Finally, I asked Steven if I could pray for him. He was delighted that I would pray. Before I prayed, I told him how Jesus wanted to transform his life, but that before He could do that, he would have to personally invite Christ into his heart and life to be his Lord and his Savior. I then began to pray.

I felt empathy toward Steven. I tried to look at him as I would one of my own sons. Tears were flowing down my cheeks as I prayed and talked with Jesus about Steven.

After closing my prayer, I gave Steven a bear hug, only to see tears streaming down his face.

That night I left for the three-hour drive back to the Los Angeles airport. In the van, my family and I talked of Steven. We silently prayed for him. As our jet took us homeward, I looked out the window into the blue vastness of earth and sky. I saw Steven. I saw those gross tattoos. I saw the mystical symbols that represented reincarnation, love, and hate. I saw the Hindu Sanskrit written on his arms. I saw the distance, the gulf between us in his eyes. I saw a tragedy-hardened face. Little tears forced their way past my eyelids. I prayed that God would find Steven and let his path cross other Christians that would love him into the Kingdom.

I have thought many times about Steven since then. I have thought of all the others whom Satan has sucked into his sickening whirlpool. I know that Steven had dabbled in New Age thought. Looking for satisfaction and meaning, Steven fell for the junk Satan pawns off as "the real thing." He offers them what appears to be a plausible way of managing their lives. He offers a deceptive system that, as usual, mingles truth and error. What he doesn't tell them is the fact that by their acceptance of this system, they assign him the rights of access to their souls. In the end, their bondage is worse than before. The freedom they seek is an illusion. Their hopes are pinned on themselves. Like gamblers playing the lottery, they give up their all in the hopes of an ever-elusive bonanza.

How does one witness to a friend or loved one caught up in the New Age movement? Are there any strategies that work?

Dr. Russell Jones, of Central Baptist Theological Seminary, Kansas City, Kans., says, "The New Age movement is ripe for intentional evangelism. It seeks a better society and world peace. It seeks peace of mind and stability. It holds some belief in life after death. It holds some belief in a supreme being. It holds to an ongoing search for answers. It seeks a formula for living and coping with society. It has all but abandoned or ignored traditional religion."[1]

Here are suggestions for developing your own working strategy of evangelism.

It is important to remember to *keep building bridges to New Age thinkers.*

Let me caution you before we go too far. Evangelizing those involved in New Age thought or activities is not easy. By the same token, it is not impossible. We should understand our primary responsibility is to witness about Jesus to everyone God sends across our pathways. Evangelism and witnessing are our responsibilities. We cannot save anyone from his sins. Only God can do that. We can, however, and we must, be Christ's witnesses in our world.

Our strategy is to remember their worth as individuals whom God created and Jesus died to redeem. Bridge building is an investment of your time, energy, and effort. It is an effort to open a dialogue, building on common ground.

Karen Hoyt of the Spiritual Counterfeits Projects lists these 10 areas in which Christians might agree with New Age thinkers:

1. Their emphasis on cooperation instead of competition (in a personal, not economic sense).

2. Their desire to protect creation, instead of exploiting and destroying earth's resources.

3. Their interest in creativity. (Christians often find themselves defending mediocrity and rigidity instead of encouraging spontaneity and creativity.)

4. Their promotion of the cause of peace in the world.

5. Their call for radical transformation—a total change of mind (although the Christian idea of the needed change is very different from the New Age movement's).

6. Their emphasis on the importance of the body and its care through proper exercise, healthy food, and good habits.

7. Their support of human potential and a positive self-image. (Christians believe people are created in God's image and therefore support human potential and the need for a positive self-image; however, they do not believe in unlimited human potential and in an unflawed self.)

8. Their position on the global village. One of the most radical changes in the last 20 years is the realization that we can no longer function as an isolated nation, politically and economically—a crisis in one country affects the whole world.

9. Their desire to work for a nontoxic environment.

10. Their use of networking. (When New Agers talk about this, some Christians get nervous and visualize world conspiracy, but the truth is that the most powerful and effective network ever is the Christian Church.)[2]

From Maurice Smith, Home Mission Board of the Southern Baptist Convention, come these excellent guidelines in witnessing:

1. Recognize that the New Age movements do advocate teachings and practices that deny or distort basic Christian beliefs.

2. An appropriate Christian response should be balanced, wholesome, and distinguished by sound biblical interpretation, reliance upon accurate information,

and genuine efforts to discuss Christian truths in clear and practical terms.

3. Insist on defining terms; yours and theirs. Call for normative Christian explanations of God, Jesus Christ, the Holy Spirit, the nature of humanity, the nature of history, the basic human problem (sin), and the solution to the basic human problem.

4. Carefully assess the worldview of people and groups you encounter. Be particularly attentive if a workshop, seminar, therapy, program or technique:

—is explained in terms of harmonizing, synergizing, integrating, or balancing energies or polarities

—emphasizes experience over belief

—involves changing your consciousness (how you perceive reality)

—teaches that you are essentially divine and you can find the solutions to your problems within yourself[3]

As Christians we believe in many of the same things our unsaved neighbors believe. We believe, however, in much more, for our beliefs are anchored to the trustworthiness of Scripture. "We have . . . a more sure word of prophecy," says Peter (2 Pet. 1:19). We know the One who holds out promise for "new heavens and a new earth" (3:13). We can introduce our friends to the One who will someday make all things new and who can effect the transformation of the new creation within the human heart and life in a twinkling of an eye.

Here is how to approach the stumbling blocks as you witness to those who are caught up in New Age thinking.

1. Start with the vitality of your personal encounter with Jesus. Tell how He transformed your life. Remember, it's show-and-tell time. If you have nothing to show, you probably have little to tell.

2. Keep in mind, you are never witnessing to win an argument or prove a point. Trust the sovereign Holy Spirit of God to do His office work in the heart and life of the

person to whom you are witnessing. He will convict and convince. Your job is to tell the Good News.

3. Keep your testimony alive. If it has been a while since you had a breakthrough experience with the Lord, repair the breach, break up the fallow ground of your heart, and experience the blessing of the Lord in a fresh newness.

4. Build on commonalities, but also hold your ground when attributing the results of your personal transformation to the Lord Jesus Christ. If your friend holds up other sources as equal to the Scriptures, politely stick to the truth that God's Word is the final expression of revelation and truth.

5. Be flexibly certain. Christians often seem rigid to New Age thinkers. They seem to be suffering from hardening of the categories. Be flexible, willing to listen, but fundamentally certain in the truth of Scripture and the validity of your own experience with the Lord. Remember the man whom Jesus healed of blindness, when questioned by the skeptics and unbelievers: "One thing I know, that, whereas I was blind, now I see" (John 9:25).

6. New Age thinkers often see us as people without passion. Before you witness, get the power and glory of God down on your soul. Immerse yourself in a devotional life-style. Never be preachy, but always be on fire.

7. Never witness out of dryness. New Age thinkers are turned off by the staid, formalized, ritualistic traditionalism of many churches. While you need to be sensitive to the Spirit, be free, loose, and easy. Take the starch out of your presentation. Let it flow in the power, love, and rhythm of the Holy Spirit.

8. Never press for a notch on your gun, but never miss an opportunity to pray. Remember, when you're praying, God is working. When you're praying, no one can argue with you. Prayer puts you and your friend immediately in the presence of God. Incredible things happen when we pray. Satan can be defeated. The powers of hell can be

bound. The believer stands on the sure, solid, high ground of spiritual communion with the Heavenly Father.

It is good to be able to communicate your beliefs in a systematic structure that is logical and makes sense. If your witness brings you to the point of serious inquiry by your New Age friend, here are eight statements that can be put in your own words to frame a working understanding about the mighty power of God to work spiritual transformation:

We believe

1. In one God—the Father, Son, and Holy Spirit.

2. That the Old and New Testament Scriptures, given by plenary inspiration, contain all truth necessary to faith and Christian living.

3. That man is born with a fallen nature, and is, therefore, inclined to evil, and that continually.

4. That the finally impenitent are hopelessly and eternally lost.

5. That the atonement through Jesus Christ is for the whole human race; and that whosoever repents and believes on the Lord Jesus Christ is justified and regenerated and saved from the dominion of sin.

6. That believers are to be sanctified wholly, subsequent to regeneration, through faith in the Lord Jesus Christ.

7. That the Holy Spirit bears witness to the new birth, and also to the entire sanctification of believers.

8. That our Lord will return, the dead will be raised, and the final judgment will take place.[4]

Be a seed planter. It is up to God to bring in the harvest. Witnessing about God's love and power in one's personal life is a starting point. Pray that God will confirm your witness with future encounters or experiences that will remind them of their need and God's availability.

The last I heard of Steven, he was still struggling to free himself by his own power from the stranglehold of sin and Satan. He moves around these days, with his little pickup, from one friend to another. He sleeps on couches, guest bedrooms when he's lucky, and in the back of his truck when things aren't going so well. I'd like to see Steven one more time. I'd like to tell him that Jesus is here and is calling for him. I'd like to tell him that Jesus still loves users and abusers, that He hasn't given up on him. I don't know if Steven can hear any of us anymore. For him, it's not a new age anymore, it's the twilight zone where he lurches from stoned to sober as he waits for the end.

"Beware lest any man spoil you through philosophy and vain deceit, after the tradition of men, after the rudiments of the world, and not after Christ. For in [Christ Jesus] dwelleth all the fulness of the Godhead bodily. And ye are complete in him, which is the head of all principality and power" (Col. 2:8-10).

Notes

Chapter 1

1. Richard Foster, *Celebration of Discipline* (San Francisco: Harper and Row, 1978), 25.

2. *Webster's New World Dictionary,* 2nd ed., s.v. "complement."

3. *Resources in Creation Spirituality* catalog (Oakland, Calif.: Friends of Creation Spirituality, Inc.), 3.

4. Ibid.

5. Maurice Smith, *Interfaith Witness Belief Bulletin,* Home Mission Board, Southern Baptist Convention. Used with permission.

6. See the works of Napoleon Hill, e.g., *Think and Grow Rich.*

7. See Napoleon Hill, *You Can Work Your Own Miracles* (New York: Fawcett Crest, 1983).

Chapter 2

1. *Webster's New World Dictionary,* 2nd ed., s.v. "pervade."

2. Sonia Nazario, "In Goddess Worship, There's Little Room for Old Patriarchy," *Wall Street Journal,* June 7, 1990.

3. Ibid.

4. Clark Roof, "The Episcopalian Goes the Way of the Dodo," *Wall Street Journal,* July 20, 1990.

5. David H. Lyman, "Being Creative," *ASTD Journal* (American Society for Training and Development, April 1989), 44-49.

6. Ibid., 45.

Chapter 3

1. See the discussion on these terms on chapter 2.

2. Maharishi World Capital of the Enlightenment, Maharishi Nagar, 210 304, UP India.

3. Institute in Creation-centered Spirituality, Mundelein College, Chicago.

4. A distinction must be drawn between those who want to protect the environment from pollution and misuse, and those who see in nature a return to some form of primitive religion.

Chapter 4

1. Used by permission.

2. From Russell Chandler, *Understanding the New Age* (Dallas: Word Publishing, 1988), 222-23.

3. Smith, *Interfaith Witness Belief Bulletin.*

4. "Agreed Statement of Belief," par. 26, *Manual of the Church of the Nazarene* (Kansas City: Nazarene Publishing House, 1989), 38-39.

Selected Bibliography

(With assistance and permission of
Rev. Maurice Smith of the Home Mission Board
Southern Baptist Convention)

Amano, J. Yutaka, and Geisler, Norman. *The Infiltration of the New Age*. Wheaton, Ill.: Tyndale House, 1989.
"A balanced critique of New Age by two Christian theologians who question the emphasis on self-deification and the occult so prominent in New Age; the authors take issue with some of the positions taken by Dave Hunt and T. A. McMahon (in *The Seduction of Christianity*)."

Chandler, Russell. *Understanding the New Age*. Dallas: Word Publishing, 1988.
"A thorough, accurate, discriminating discussion by a Christian journalist with theological training; well documented, very readable by Christians and by New Age adherents; has an excellent glossary. Chandler's suggestions for Christians are helpful but not exhaustive. This is certainly one of the best books on New Age. Highly recommended."

Cumbey, Constance. *The Hidden Dangers of the Rainbow: The New Age Movement and Our Coming Age of Barbarism*. Shreveport, La.: Huntington House, 1983.
"This book, which has been very influential in stimulating the interest of evangelical Christians to be aware of New Age, should nevertheless be read cautiously. The author sometimes bases her discussion on faulty premises and makes generalizations that can be questioned. This should not be the only source you read on the New Age Movements."

Groothuis, Douglas R. *Unmasking the New Age*. Downers Grove, Ill.: InterVarsity Press, 1986.
"One of the best books to help Christians understand the New Age; clear, balanced, factual, and thorough. The author has a particularly useful discussion and chart showing the

differences between New Age systems and secular humanism. Recommended."

——*Confronting the New Age.* Downers Grove, Ill.: InterVarsity Press, 1988.

"Groothuis suggests definite steps for Christians to take in witnessing to New Age adherents, identifying New Age influences in business seminars, school curriculum, pop psychology, therapy, and music. Written in a popular style, with good documentation, this book is insightful and helpful, although you may not agree with all the author's interpretation and application of Christian theology."

Hoyt, Karen, and Yamamoto, J. Isamu, eds. *The New Age Rage.* Old Tappan, N.J.: Fleming H. Revell Co., 1987.

"This valuable work by the staff of the Spiritual Counterfeits Project contrasts New Age world views with biblical world views and shows how New Age Movements have influenced society and even the Church. In a cohesive, sensible fashion, the authors stress the importance of understanding and combating the negative ideas represented in these loosely linked movements. This is one of the very best books for Christians to read to have a good grasp of the rationale and philosophy of New Age."

Lutzer, Erwin, and DeVries, John F. *Satan's Strategy for the New Age.* Wheaton, Ill.: Victor Books, 1989.

"Describes New Age deception as Satan's 'four spiritual flaws,' pantheism, reincarnation, moral relativism, and esotericism. Written in a readable, popular style, this book offers an interesting and different approach to helping Christians respond to New Age. Should be helpful."

Miller, Elliot. *A Crash Course on the New Age Movement: Describing and Evaluating a Growing Social Force.* Grand Rapids: Baker Book House, 1989.

"An excellent survey and critique of New Age ideology; one of the best treatments from a Christian viewpoint. The author, who formerly embraced New Age beliefs, is now editor of the *Christian Research Journal.*"